Fall in New Hampshire

TABLE OF CONTENTS

1. Colorful autumn leaves, behind Indian Head Resort.
2. Red and orange maple leaves, on side of road.
3. Bretton Woods Resort within the town of Carroll.
4. The Flume Gorge.
5. Waterfalls in the Flume Gorge.
6. Pumpkin and rocking chairs on front porch.
7. Covered bridge.
8. Pumpkins and decorative mums in front of Breton Woods Resort.
9. Horses grazing.
10. Blue heron on shore on pond.
11. Mums and pumpkins with view of mountain.

Author Charles Elias.

Resides in Sandown, New Hampshire and enjoys writing his stories and is the Author of:

Charlie Works at The Grocery Store

              &

Charlie's Spooky Halloween

Both books have been made into coloring books and can be purchased online.

Charles also had a wonderful time taking these photographs in New England's White Mountains.